ALEXI SARGEANT

SAINTLY CREATURES

14 TALES OF ANIMALS AND THEIR HOLY COMPANIONS

ILLUSTRATED BY
ANITA BARGHIGIANI

ALEXI SARGEANT

SAINTLY CREATURES

14 TALES OF ANIMALS AND THEIR HOLY COMPANIONS

ILLUSTRATED BY
ANITA BARGHIGIANI

Published by Word on Fire Votive, an imprint of
Word on Fire, Elk Grove Village, IL 60007
© 2023 by Word on Fire Catholic Ministries
Printed in Italy
All rights reserved

Cover design, typesetting, and interior art direction by Nicolas Fredrickson and Rozann Lee
Editing by Haley Stewart
Copyediting by James O'Neil

No part of this book may be used or reproduced in any manner whatsoever without written permission, except in the case of brief quotations in critical articles or reviews. For more information, contact Word on Fire Catholic Ministries, PO Box 97330, Washington, DC 20090-7330 or email contact@wordonfire.org.

First published September 2023
Reprinted October 2023, March 2024

ISBN: 978-1-68578-989-3

Library of Congress Control Number: 2022943398

To my wife, Leah Sargeant. Thank you for your encouragement and support every step of the way!

—A.S.

A mia nonna Fiorenza e al suo infinito amore per tutta la famiglia.

To my grandmother Fiorenza for her endless love for all our family.

—A.B.

Contents

7   *The Boar and Saint Brigid*

11 *The Mice and Saint Martin de Porres*

15 *The Wolf and Saint Francis of Assisi*

19 *The Horse and Saint José Sánchez del Río*

23 *The Sheep and Saint Germaine Cousin*

27 *The Tiger and Blessed James Heo In-baek*

31 *The Geese and Saint Werburgh*

35 *The Great Gray Dog and Saint John Bosco*

39 *The Bees and Saint Rita*

43 *The Hyena and Saint Macarius*

47 *The Ravens and Saint Meinrad*

51 *The Lion and Saint Mary of Egypt*

55 *The Whale and Saint Brendan*

59 *The Pets of Blessed Carlo Acutis*

The Boar and Saint Brigid

A wild boar ran for his life through an oak forest of fifth-century Ireland. The beast must have been a frightening sight: bristling black hair, fierce curving tusks, and four thunderous hooves pounding through the undergrowth. But just then, it was the boar who was frightened! He was injured and a hunting party was on his tail: dogs baying for his blood and men on horseback readying weapons. And the hunters were gaining on the boar. Soon there would be nowhere left to run.

But as the boar charged through a gate and drew closer to a cluster of wooden buildings, the hunters came to a halt, reining in their horses and calling off their dogs. The boar, run ragged from the chase, was relieved. But why had his pursuers stopped their hunt? The creature had unknowingly entered the grounds of Kildare Abbey.

The hunters did not want to charge onto the abbey's hallowed grounds, but they had not given up their pursuit. They believed they only needed to wait for the monks and nuns living at the abbey to chase the boar away, and then they could seize their prey. But the hunters did not count on the reaction of a saintly woman of Kildare.

This beautiful abbey had been founded by Brigid, who presided there as abbess. Brigid had been born not long after Saint Patrick brought the Christian faith to Ireland. Her mother was a slave who had been converted by Patrick's preaching. But her father did not accept this new faith. He was a pagan chieftain who claimed Brigid's mother as property. Her father even named little Brigid after a pagan goddess.

But God was with Brigid. From her infancy, her life was marked by miracles. There was one time when neighbors thought her mother's house was on fire, but it was actually a blazing light that surrounded the sleeping baby Brigid. The druids—the pagan religious leaders in Ireland—might have thought she had magic powers. But Brigid, raised as a Christian, always knew the miracles came from God.

Brigid's generosity often surprised and sometimes infuriated the powerful chieftains and kings she encountered. She spent time as a servant at her father's house, and when a beggar came asking for alms, she gave him her father's jeweled sword. Brigid's father was very angry, but she calmly explained that nothing he had was too good to be given away for Jesus' sake.

At the court of the King of Leinster, Brigid admired the harps hanging on the wall. The king told her that, sadly, no one at court could play the instruments. Brigid said a prayer over the hands of some court servants, and they took up the harps and began to play beautiful music! The grateful king offered Brigid any reward she would like to choose. Rather than gold or jewels, she chose to relieve the suffering of others and immediately asked the king to release all those held in his prisons.

Though her father wanted to marry her off, Brigid knew she was called to take the veil and consecrate her life to God as a religious sister.

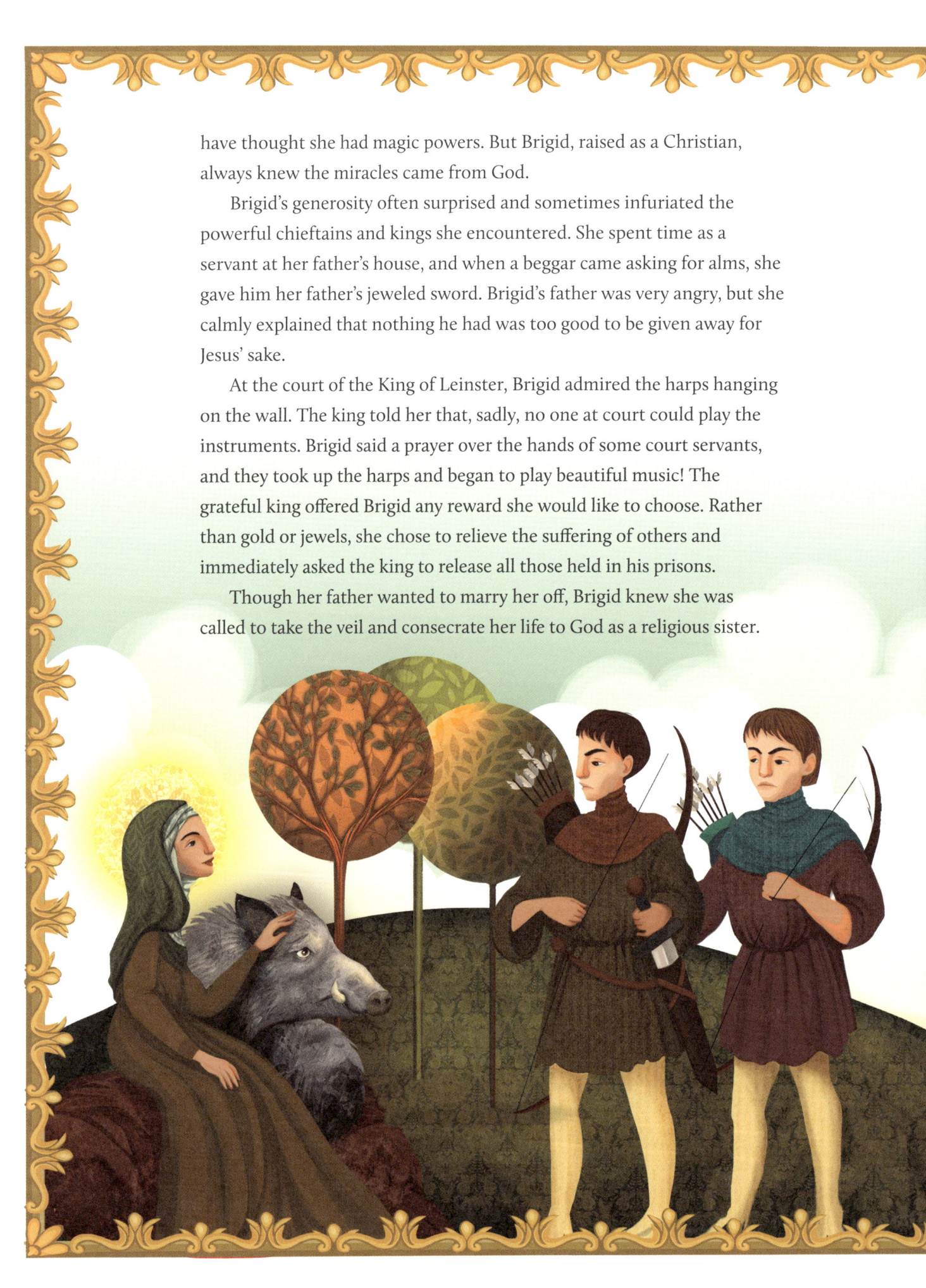

She gathered a group of companions and founded Kildare Abbey, which eventually grew into a double monastery with a building for men and a building for women. She spread the faith through generosity, missionary zeal, and miracles of healing.

On the day the boar came to Kildare Abbey, Brigid was outside tending to the abbey's livestock. She spotted the wounded animal as he panted to catch his breath. Pitying the boar, she said to him, "Poor creature, have you come to the house of the Lord in search of safety? You have done well." She offered the animal a drink of water and sent word to the hunters that the boar would receive sanctuary at the abbey. She would protect him from harm.

The hunters were confused. They sent a message back, saying, "Abbess, it is only an animal, not some penitent criminal in search of sanctuary. Can we please have our boar back?" But Brigid was firm. "I will offer Christ's mercy to any who run to it at Kildare Abbey, whether on four legs or two." The disappointed hunting party rode away that day without their prey.

Brigid tended to the injured and frightened boar and brought it to join her herd of domesticated pigs. At first the other animals squealed and ran from this wild creature, and the boar bristled with suspicion at this strange new herd. But Brigid spoke words of blessing over the newcomer, and he became quite tame, living out the rest of his days among the contented farm animals of Kildare Abbey.

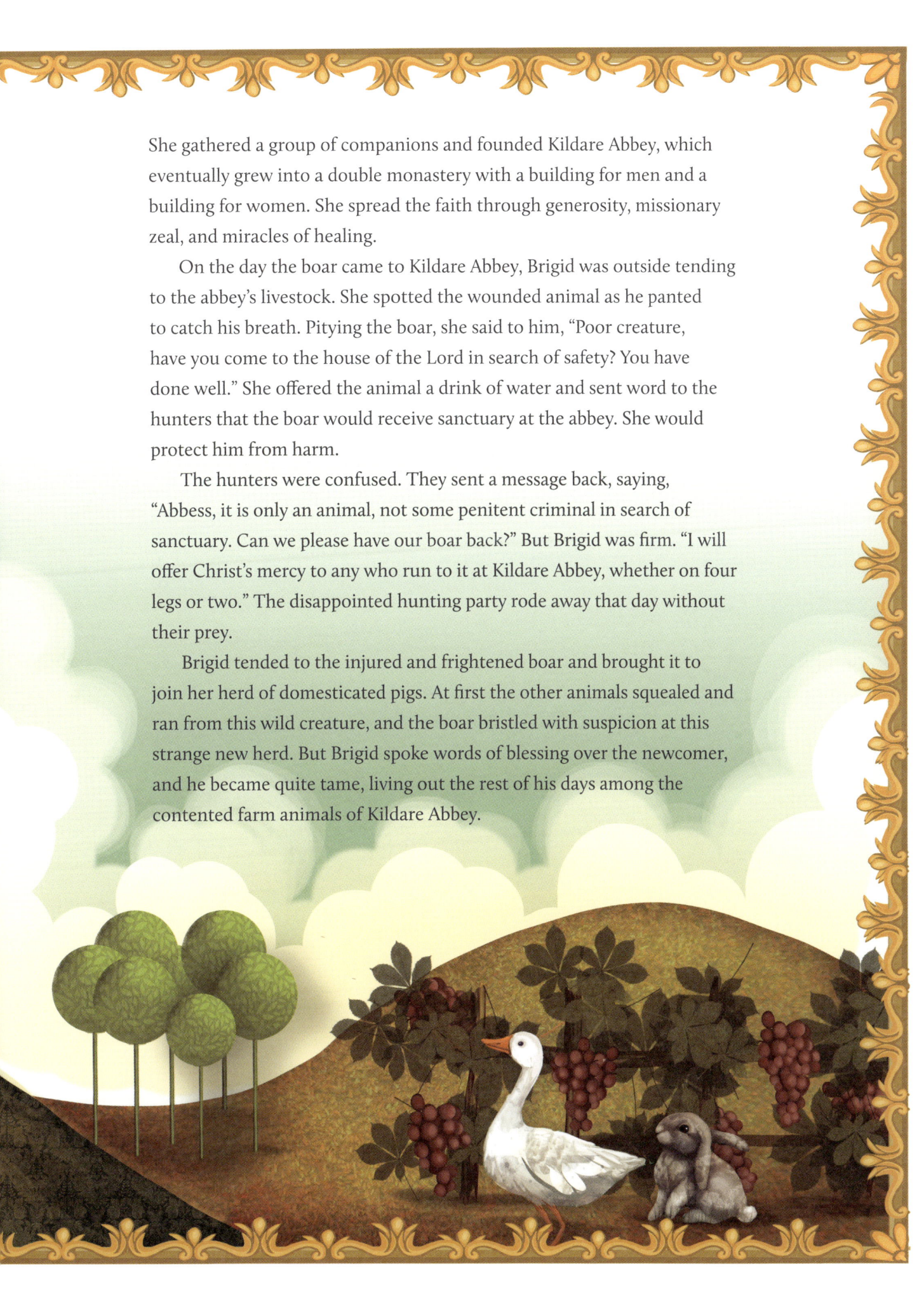

The Mice and Saint Martin de Porres

In the 1600s, a family of mice in Peru thought they had found a great place to live. They sneaked into Holy Rosary Priory in Lima, scurrying through the nooks and crannies, gnawing holes in the friars' robes, and even eating the sacred linens in the sacristy. That was all very well for the mice, but the friars soon had enough of these unwelcome guests. The monastery decided to get rid of the uninvited creatures with traps and poison. But, fortunately for the mice, a miracle took place before the traps could spring.

Who performed this miracle? It was a man who, like the mice, had not always been welcome in the places he wanted to call home. Martin was the son of a Spanish nobleman. He grew up in poverty with his younger sister and his mother, a woman of African and Native Peruvian descent. For many years, Martin's wealthy father ignored Martin and his sister and did not tell anyone they were his son and daughter. It seems he never married Martin's mother.

From a young age, Martin had a heart for helping others. He learned the basics of medicine from a barber-surgeon. He gave money to the poor, even though he had little enough of it to give. And he developed a great love for God and wished to join a religious order as a friar.

At age fifteen, Martin took up residence at the Holy Rosary Priory of the Dominican Order. But he was not allowed to become a brother there and was instead assigned only the lowliest chores. Why wasn't he allowed to be a brother? Because of the unjust laws in Peru, which prevented anyone with an African or Native Peruvian parent from joining a religious order. Martin decided he would perform the chores he was given—cooking, cleaning, taking care of the sick—and trust God to work out the rest.

It took nine years, but Martin was finally invited to make vows as a Dominican brother. The prior, moved by Martin's faithful service, decided to disregard the unjust law. But there were three hundred other brothers at the priory, and not all of them were kind to Martin. Some made fun of him or spoke hatefully to him because of the color of his skin and the circumstances of his birth. They were looking at him with the eyes of the world, not the eyes of Christ.

But Martin was not like these brothers. He treated everyone with love and generosity. He begged for money to help families in need of food, clothes, or dowries for their daughters. He treated enslaved people with the same respect given to rich noblemen. And he was good to animals as well, working with his sister to shelter stray dogs and cats. The mice of the priory did not know it, but they had fallen into good hands with Martin.

Instead of using traps or poison, Martin reached into a cupboard and pulled out a single mouse. The mouse must have been surprised, even

terrified, to be lifted up in the Dominican brother's brown hands. But Martin spoke gently and softly to the mouse, and soon it grew calm, as if it could tell he meant it no harm. "Little brother," Martin said to the mouse, "you are eating things we need in order to serve the Lord and take care of the sick! But I will make a deal with you. Take your family and leave our cupboards, and I will feed you once a day—outdoors."

Here was the miracle: the mouse seemed to understand Martin's words! Martin set the mouse down and it scurried away, followed by dozens and dozens of other mice, who came streaming from all the nooks and crannies of the priory. They assembled in the garden, where Martin, true to his word, brought them some food. The mice burrowed holes in the garden to create a new home where they would not disturb the friars. Every day Martin offered them scraps from the kitchen, and his friends the mice never invaded the priory again.

The Wolf and Saint Francis of Assisi

The town of Gubbio was full of fear. People barred their doors, spoke in whispers, and pulled their children close. A terror stalked the region: a great wolf, huge, fierce, and hungry. At first he had preyed on their livestock, but then he started to attack people as well. Many townspeople became afraid to venture beyond the walls of Gubbio because the wolf had grown bold enough to hunt any humans he saw.

Who would free the citizens of Gubbio from this terror? As it happened, it was not a band of hunters or a knight in shining armor. Instead, a little friar wearing ragged robes set out confidently to confront the beast, with a few hardy brothers accompanying him.

The townspeople urged the friar not to be so foolish. The wolf would surely eat him if he approached. But the friar was undeterred, and a crowd of curious townspeople followed at a distance—ready to run if the wolf ate him up and then wanted dessert.

The band of friars and onlookers set out for the lair where the wolf was rumored to lurk. Sure enough, the beast came bounding forth, letting out a ferocious howl and then charging at the little friar with his great sharp teeth bared. The townspeople braced themselves to see the wolf gobble up their unlikely champion.

Instead, the friar made the sign of the cross and commanded, "Come here, Brother Wolf! In the name of Jesus Christ, do no harm to me or any other." Miraculously, the wolf obeyed the command. He closed his jaws, approached the friar meekly, and settled down at the feet of Brother Francis.

Who was this strange little friar who could tame wild beasts? Francis grew up in Assisi, a town of Italy, in the late 1100s. He was the son of a wealthy merchant and spent his youth wearing fine clothes and spending money lavishly. But when he was a young man, he had a vision from God that led him to change his life entirely. He renounced his inheritance, embraced a life of poverty, and began traveling the countryside to serve the poor and preach the Gospel. Eventually, Francis founded an order of friars to live this unusual life alongside him.

Francis was famous for his love of all God's creation. He addressed everything as his brother or sister, even the sun and moon. He had a special way with animals and once preached a sermon to a flock of birds about God's love for them. And so the wolf, who seemed like a terrible monster to the people of Gubbio, was simply "Brother Wolf" to Francis—a creature of God's who might, like a sinful man, be transformed.

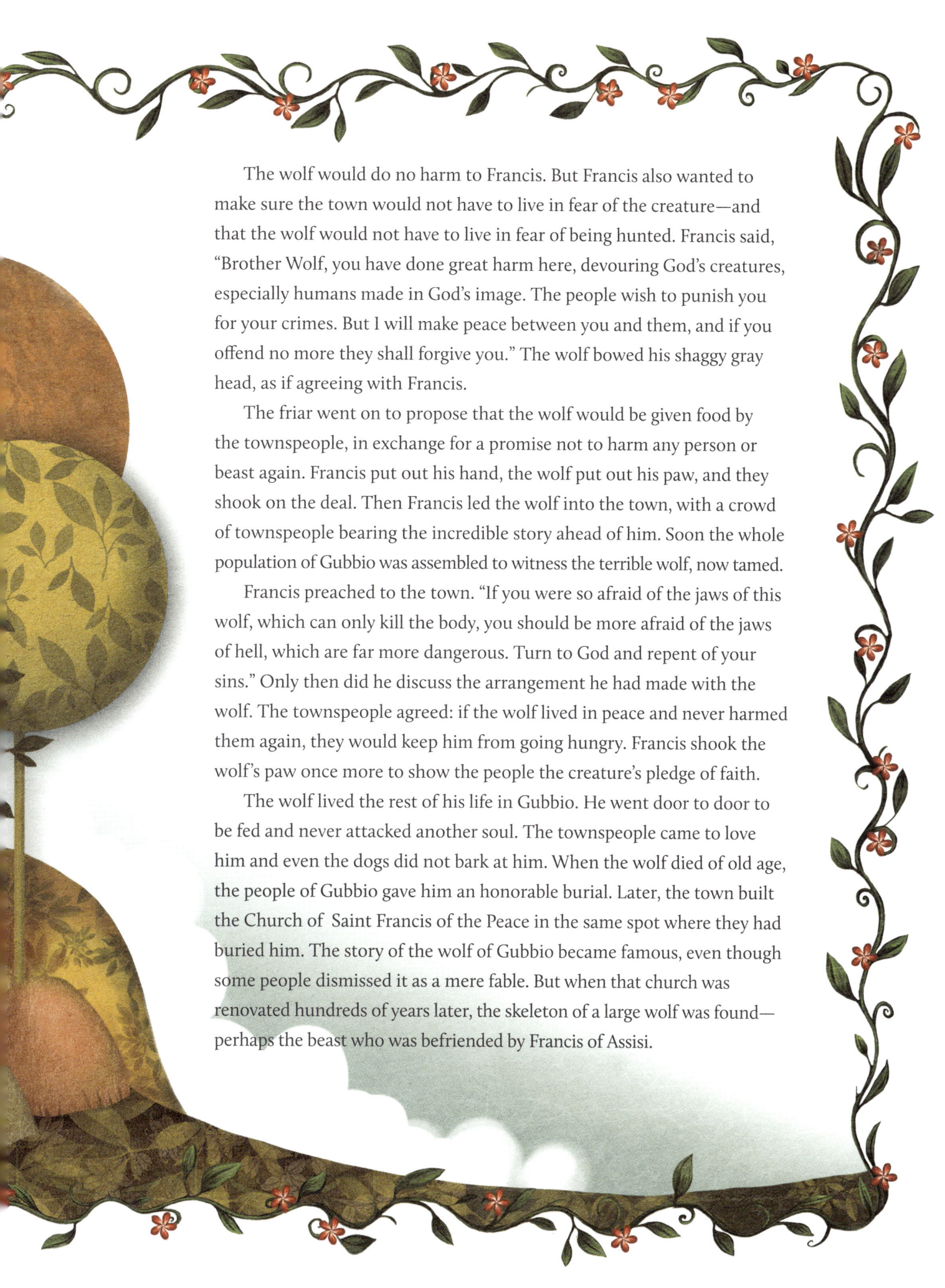

The wolf would do no harm to Francis. But Francis also wanted to make sure the town would not have to live in fear of the creature—and that the wolf would not have to live in fear of being hunted. Francis said, "Brother Wolf, you have done great harm here, devouring God's creatures, especially humans made in God's image. The people wish to punish you for your crimes. But I will make peace between you and them, and if you offend no more they shall forgive you." The wolf bowed his shaggy gray head, as if agreeing with Francis.

The friar went on to propose that the wolf would be given food by the townspeople, in exchange for a promise not to harm any person or beast again. Francis put out his hand, the wolf put out his paw, and they shook on the deal. Then Francis led the wolf into the town, with a crowd of townspeople bearing the incredible story ahead of him. Soon the whole population of Gubbio was assembled to witness the terrible wolf, now tamed.

Francis preached to the town. "If you were so afraid of the jaws of this wolf, which can only kill the body, you should be more afraid of the jaws of hell, which are far more dangerous. Turn to God and repent of your sins." Only then did he discuss the arrangement he had made with the wolf. The townspeople agreed: if the wolf lived in peace and never harmed them again, they would keep him from going hungry. Francis shook the wolf's paw once more to show the people the creature's pledge of faith.

The wolf lived the rest of his life in Gubbio. He went door to door to be fed and never attacked another soul. The townspeople came to love him and even the dogs did not bark at him. When the wolf died of old age, the people of Gubbio gave him an honorable burial. Later, the town built the Church of Saint Francis of the Peace in the same spot where they had buried him. The story of the wolf of Gubbio became famous, even though some people dismissed it as a mere fable. But when that church was renovated hundreds of years later, the skeleton of a large wolf was found—perhaps the beast who was befriended by Francis of Assisi.

The Horse and Saint José Sánchez del Río

Amidst the frenzy of a battlefield, a lone horse galloped furiously. Though his rider was only a boy of fourteen, the horse trusted him to guide them safely through the chaos. All around, bullets were flying, smoke was billowing, and soldiers were stumbling around the bodies of the wounded and fallen. The rider held aloft a flag. It was green, white, and red, the colors of his country, Mexico. On the flag was an image of Mary as Our Lady of Guadalupe and the words *Viva Cristo Rey*—Long Live Christ the King!

The horse looked ahead and saw another horse, but that one would run no more. The fallen horse had been struck by an enemy's shot, and his rider was now on foot, calling orders to the panicked troops. But they were scattering fast, and the enemy was closing in. The boy spurred his mount toward the unhorsed rider. He called down, "My general!" The general looked up at his young flagbearer, who continued, "Take my horse and save yourself. You are more needed for this cause than I."

The general reluctantly agreed. The rider leapt down, and the horse whinnied in confusion. The boy gave his horse a last pat. "Do not worry about me, my faithful friend. Get the general to safety!" Mounted on the boy's horse, the general galloped away from the losing battle, escaping capture so he could fight another day. The boy who had given up his horse fought valiantly but was taken prisoner by the opposing army.

That rider was José Sánchez del Río. When war broke out in 1926, this ordinary Mexican boy wanted to fight for his faith. The government of Mexico was trying to suppress the Catholic Church. They started by punishing priests for wearing clerical garb in public and imprisoning priests who criticized the government. Then they began seizing churches and closing monasteries, convents, and religious schools. When peaceful protests were met with further persecution, Catholics took up arms to fight back.

José's older brothers, Macario and Miguel, joined the Catholic rebel soldiers, known as the Cristeros. But their mother did not want José to fight—after all, he was only twelve years old at the time. He pleaded with her, saying that Catholics should accept the risks of this war knowing that it was in the service of God. "Mamá, do not let me lose the opportunity to gain heaven so easily and so soon."

His mother relented, but the Cristero general was also resistant to bringing one so young into battle. Eventually, the general allowed José to

be his flagbearer. And that is how, two years later, José came to be carrying a flag and riding a horse into a losing battle. José gave up his horse to serve the general. He would give up his life to serve Christ the King.

The government's troops imprisoned José in a makeshift cell at a local church they had seized. In fact, it was the very church where José had been baptized as a baby: the Church of Saint James the Apostle in Sahuayo, Mexico. His captors ordered him to renounce his faith in Christ, but he refused. He remembered what his Baptism meant.

Without receiving a real trial, José was sentenced to death. One of his aunts smuggled him Holy Communion while he was waiting for his execution. The soldiers tortured their young prisoner and forced him to walk to his place of martyrdom on wounded feet. But their cruelty could not defeat the young man's courage. All the way, he prayed the Rosary and called out his battle cry of faith: "*Viva Cristo Rey y Santa María de Guadalupe!*"—Long Live Christ the King and Holy Mary of Guadalupe!

The Sheep and Saint Germaine Cousin

In a sleepy French town in the late 1500s, a bell was tolling, summoning the faithful to Mass. The sound of the bell echoed through the houses of the rich and the poor, through farmhouses and workshops. It reached a lonely field close by a dark wood where a young shepherd girl tended a flock of sheep. At the sound of the bell, the girl smiled. She planted her shepherd's staff upright in the ground and addressed the sheep. "I must go to Mass to see Jesus. But do not be afraid, my wooly friends. I am entrusting you to the care of my guardian angel."

The sheep gave a few parting bleats as the shepherd girl, Germaine Cousin, made her way back to the village for church. Though the field was far from the village and hungry wolves stalked the dark woods, the sheep felt calm and safe. Germaine had done this many times—every day, in fact. She had a simple faith in Jesus, the Good Shepherd. She knew he would help watch over her sheep. And the sheep had learned to trust as well.

Germaine Cousin's life had been far from easy. She was born with a deformed right hand that she could not move and a disease called scrofula that caused bumps to grow on the skin of her neck. Her mother died when she was very young, and her father remarried a woman named Hortense, who treated Germaine terribly.

Hortense acted like Germaine was a servant instead of a daughter. She gave her only scraps to eat and encouraged her other children to shun their stepsister. She would not let Germaine sleep in the house, claiming she was protecting the other children from her disease. Instead, Germaine had to sleep in the barn. On cold winter nights, the only warmth to be found in the barn was that of the wooly sheep.

Despite the evil way she was treated, Germaine grew up with a gentle spirit and an abiding love for God. She was never allowed to go to school, but she learned the Rosary and prayed it on a simple knotted string. Her stepmother assigned her the task of shepherding the sheep, perhaps cruelly hoping a wolf would come along and finish off the underfed and sickly shepherd girl. But Germaine not only took care of the sheep—she also taught the children of the village about God.

At first it was only children and sheep who appreciated Germaine's goodness. The other villagers snickered at the piety of this girl with the strange hand and skin. But soon there began to be stories of miracles surrounding Germaine. Someone reported that Germaine had been walking from her flock to the church when she came to an overflowing river. The flooding was so high that the bridge could not be used. Germaine calmly made the sign of the cross, and the waters parted to let her get to Mass.

Eventually, the people of the village realized that Germaine was a holy young woman and that they had been wrong to mock her. They started to listen to her, and some tried to make up for their previous treatment of her. Even Germaine's father and stepmother realized that they needed to change their behavior. They invited Germaine back into the house, but the young woman declined, content with the simplicity of her life.

Germaine died at the age of twenty-two. She had never been healthy, and her stepmother's harsh mistreatment had surely weakened her body. People who had seen the beauty of her life thought she might be a saint, and they began to pray for her intercession and receive miracles in response. But the humble sheep were the first to know how blessed Saint Germaine was. Through her years of going to Mass and entrusting them to her guardian angel, not one lamb of her flock had been lost.

The Tiger and Blessed James Heo In-baek

In a cold mountain cave, three men huddled together in fear. They were Korean Catholics, and they were fleeing from government officers who wanted to arrest and kill them. Even though Christians had been living in Korea for almost a hundred years, in the mid-1800s the ruling dynasty was seeking to stamp out the faith. One of the men, James Heo In-baek, had been arrested and tortured once before for being Catholic. Now, he and his two companions prayed together in nervous whispers. Then a noise from outside the cave broke the stillness of the gloomy night.

The men paused in their prayer. Could their persecutors have found their hiding place? But the noise sounded more like a low growl from an animal than a group of armed men. James Heo In-baek approached the mouth of the cave and had to stifle a gasp. Looming over him was the bulk of a massive tiger. The great striped cat took a step toward him. The three Catholics had accidentally taken refuge in the tiger's den!

All three had expected practicing the faith to be dangerous, but not quite like this. One of the men, Peter Yi Yang-deung, was the catechist who taught the faith to Christians in the village of Jukryeong. Another, Luke Kim Jong-ryun, had been born to a noble family, then fled to Jukryeong for refuge when persecution broke out. And what of the third man, the one staring down the tiger?

Heo In-baek was born to a peasant family and took the baptismal name "James" when he converted in his mid-twenties. He taught the faith to his wife, Pak Jo-i, and their children. He lived a humble life, supporting his family with carpentry work and giving generously to the poor and the sick.

When the last round of persecutions broke out, James was arrested, tortured, and kept in prison for eight months. But this terrible treatment could not keep him from professing his faith in God. He was only released when the king ordered that the persecution stop.

Upon his release, James sought out other Christians in order to live in community. He joined Peter Yi Yang-deung and Luke Kim Jong-ryun in Jukryeong, and the three became friends. Meanwhile, the king, who was friendly to Christians, died and a new ruler took power. The new government revived the merciless suppression of the faith. For a while, the three men were safe in their remote village. But when the government officers heard about their community, they knew they were in danger. Now they found themselves hiding in a mountain cave—James locking eyes with a tiger that was so close he could feel its warm breath!

As the fearsome cat stalked into the cave, James made the sign of the cross and spoke to it: "We are just passersby, not thieves. Please forgive us for trespassing in your cave. Would you let us shelter here a little longer? We will return the cave to you, with our gratitude, when the danger to us has passed." Remarkably, the tiger seemed sympathetic to the Christians'

plight. Instead of devouring James and his companions, it turned around and left the cave.

During the nerve-racking days and nights spent in the cave, James and the other two men would sometimes hear the tiger's growl again, its deep rumble echoing through the mountains. But they were no longer afraid. It was as if the tiger were standing guard, warning other beasts away from the cave. When the men finally left, they thanked God for the mercy of the tiger.

The government was less merciful. Eventually, all three of the Christians were arrested. As he was being led away, James said to his family, "Pray for me, and think of the story of the martyrdom of Saint Barbara." Like martyrs of old, and like his two companions, James went to his death proclaiming his faith in God and calling aloud to Jesus and Mary. Afterward, his wife, Pak Jo-i, found his body and those of his two companions and gave them Christian burials in secret.

The Geese and Saint Werburgh

A great flock of geese was causing trouble in the village of Weedon in England. The birds were descending on the farms and convent fields, eating up the wheat planted by peasants and nuns. The geese honked and pecked at anyone who tried to get in their way as they attacked the crops. The villagers were scared and angry because the geese were endangering their harvest. They turned to the abbess of the convent for help.

The abbess, a woman named Werburgh, was not intimidated by the geese. Brandishing a shepherd's staff and accompanied by the abbey steward and some servants, she fearlessly drove the whole flock of geese into an empty stable. "Bar the doors," she said. "The geese shall stay here overnight as punishment for their thievery. In the morning we will send them on their way."

The abbess was confident she could put an end to the village's goose problem. But her steward had his own plans. Through the slats of the stable, he spied an especially plump goose. His stomach growled as he imagined the taste of goose stew. When no one was looking, he went into the stable, grabbed the goose he wanted, and rushed out, slamming the door behind him. He muffled the goose's honks of surprise as he hurried home. There he killed, plucked, and cooked the goose for dinner.

When the abbess came to let the geese out in the morning, it was clear something was wrong. The geese were flapping their wings furiously and making great honking noises of dismay. They seemed to be begging the good woman for something. The abbess eventually understood what was upsetting the birds, and she set out to make things right.

Werburgh was no stranger to the difficulties of leadership. Her family was full of both royalty and saints. She was born a princess of the Anglo-Saxon kingdom of Mercia. Her mother was a saint who converted her father, the leader of a fierce, warlike people. He became the first Christian king of Mercia. Werburgh was considered very beautiful and received many offers of marriage, but what she wanted was to become a nun and dedicate her life to God. Her father allowed her to do so, and she joined the Abbey of Ely, a convent that had been founded by her great-aunt—another saint!

When her father died, her uncle became king. He asked her to leave her simple life at Ely and take charge of all the convents in his domain to help bring more order to them. She worked hard to help improve the existing convents and founded several new ones, always relying on God's

guidance. Her nuns loved her for her tender and motherly care. Dealing with the geese in Weedon was just one example of Werburgh's genius for solving a convent's problems.

The perceptive abbess called the abbey servants before her and demanded answers about the missing goose. The steward, ashamed, confessed what he had done. Werburgh looked at him sternly. "Bring me," she said, "the feathers and bones of the bird that has been eaten."

The steward hurried home and gathered up the leftover bones and plucked feathers of the goose, all the while wondering what Werburgh meant to do. He deposited the sad scraps at Werburgh's feet. She made the sign of the cross, said a prayer, and commanded the goose bones and feathers to be whole and live. Miraculously, the goose was restored, good as new and plump as ever! The rest of the flock honked in celebration and thanks.

Werburgh admonished the birds to trouble the village no more, then released them to fly free. It is said that, to this day, the village of Weedon has had no more trouble with geese.

The Great Gray Dog and Saint John Bosco

As the sun went down on the Italian countryside, a priest was lost in thought as he walked back to the city of Turin. Just as he reached a place where the road sloped downward, his solitude was disturbed by the sound of footsteps behind him. He turned and saw a man charging toward him, hefting a club. It was an ambush!

The priest fought to defend himself from his attacker. He did not know why this man wanted to hurt him, but this was not his first time being attacked. There were people who hated his good work and his preaching of the faith. He landed a blow that knocked his attacker down. But then a dozen more men charged from where they had been lying in wait at the bottom of the slope, brandishing clubs and surrounding the poor priest. The situation seemed dire.

Suddenly, a deep growl sounded. Out of nowhere, an enormous dog had appeared. His fur was gray and his teeth were bared. The dog snarled and sprang around the priest, scattering the attackers. The animal's ferocity was such that the men might have thought a wolf had leapt on them.

"Call him off! Call him off!" pleaded the cowering ambushers. "Let them go, Grigio," said the priest. The gray dog stopped leaping at the attackers but instead stood on guard, staring them down. The thwarted band of men beat a hasty retreat into the darkness. The rescued man, Father John Bosco, patted the great gray dog's head. "Thank you for saving me once again, Grigio."

John Bosco, often known as "Don Bosco," was an Italian priest who was born in 1815. He was dedicated to helping poor boys and young men lead good lives. He gave a home to boys who had nowhere else to go at the Oratory of Saint Francis de Sales, where he helped them learn to do useful work as shoemakers and tailors. The boys loved him for his kind and fatherly heart. But there were some people who hated John because he spoke the truth with courage and criticized anti-Catholic groups.

Time after time, when John Bosco was in danger, a great gray dog would appear and help him. John named the dog "Grigio," meaning "gray." At first, Grigio merely turned up to accompany John through a dangerous part of town. When he reached the Oratory, the dog would slip away.

Grigio would intervene more dramatically when evildoers attacked the good priest. Once a man fired a gun at John. The bullets missed, and Grigio charged out of nowhere and sank his teeth into the shooter, who ran away screaming. Another time, two assailants grabbed John and threw a sack over his head. Grigio leaped and seized one attacker by the throat. When the other fled in terror, John told Grigio to release the poor, whimpering man whose neck he held in his jaws.

John's mother, Margherita, who assisted him in his work, always found Grigio's wolflike appearance frightening. Still, she was grateful for his protective presence. On one occasion, John wanted to leave the Oratory to attend to an urgent matter. His mother begged him not to go. She had a feeling that this dark night was especially dangerous. John tried to reassure her and said that he would have some of the students accompany him. As they tried to set out, however, they found Grigio blocking the gate. The students tried to shoo the dog away, and one even gave him a playful kick. Grigio responded with a resounding bark. Margherita said, "Don't go out, John. If you won't listen to me, at least listen to that dog! He's got more sense than you do." Margherita and Grigio were right. A quarter of an hour later, a neighbor arrived to warn John that dangerous men were lurking near the Oratory, planning to seize John. Once again, Grigio had rescued the priest.

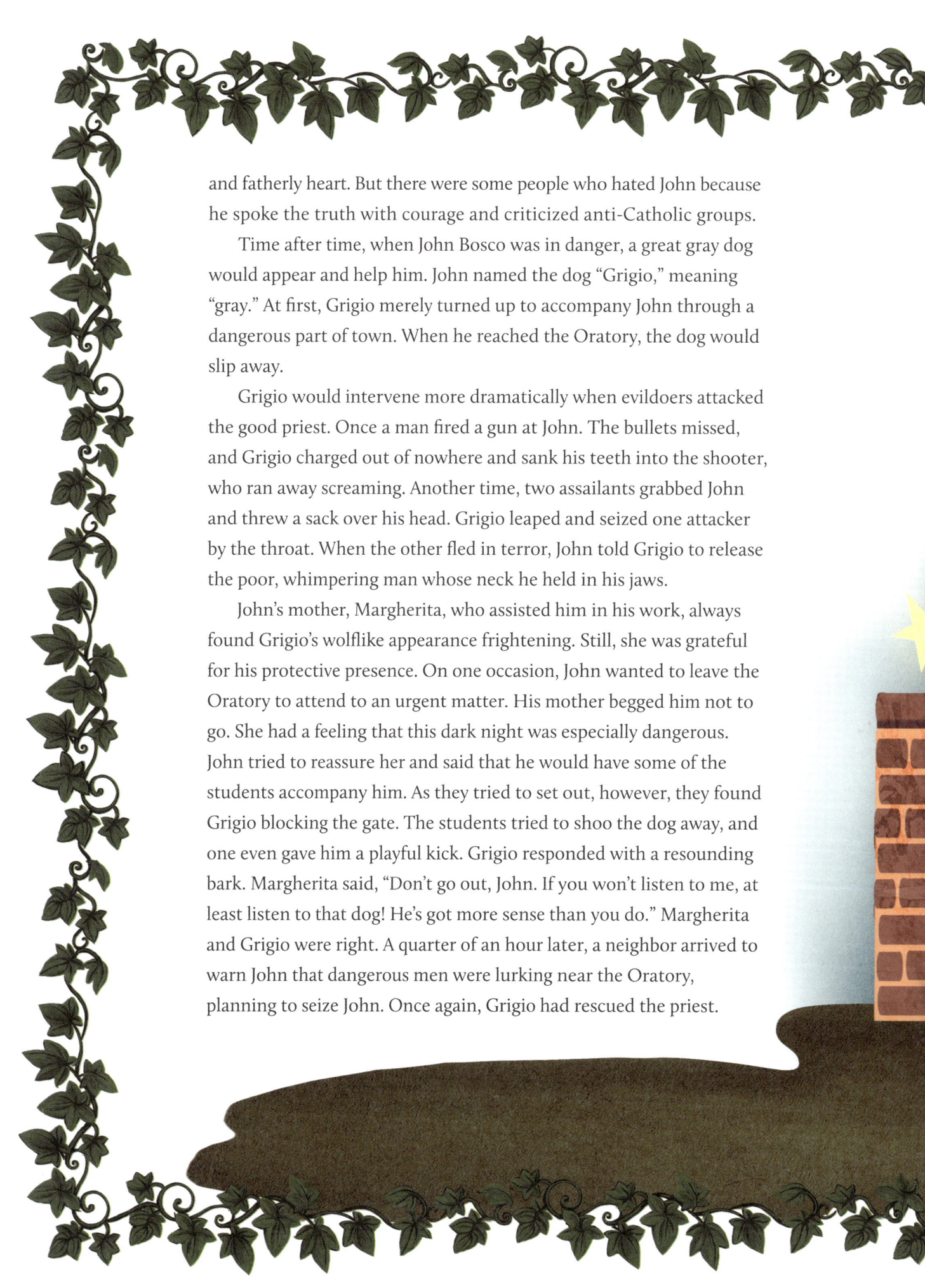

Grigio was a very mysterious savior. He was never seen to eat, and he appeared to help John on many occasions over the course of thirty years. Was he an earthly dog at all, or a guardian angel appearing in a four-footed form? All we know for sure is that he was a truly loyal and stalwart friend to a kind-hearted priest in need.

The Bees and Saint Rita

"I can't believe it!" "Have you ever seen anything like it?" Family members and curious neighbors clustered around the newborn baby girl's cradle. They were not amazed to see a calmly sleeping five-day-old baby, whom they had seen baptized the day before in the local church. What had them all abuzz was an extraordinary sight: a swarm of bees was flying around the infant, without seeming to disturb her at all.

These bees were not everyday bees. They were pure white, and they were landing on the little baby's lips and sometimes flying in and out of her mouth. No one dared to shoo them away because everyone thought such miraculous creatures must be a sign from God. The bees dispersed on their own, and the family was left to debate the meaning of the snow-colored swarm. Did the bees represent the virtues of industry and devotion?

The baby was Margherita Lotti, also known as Rita. She grew up in Cascia, Italy, at the end of the 1300s. In her seventy-five years of life, she experienced great suffering and great grace. Perhaps the bees that appeared the day after her Baptism were a sign of how her life would be full of the sting of the cross and the honey of the Resurrection.

Rita loved God from a young age, and her dearest wish was to join a convent of religious sisters. However, her parents arranged for her to marry a wealthy nobleman named Paolo Mancini. They may have believed they were doing the right thing for their beloved daughter, but the arranged marriage was not a happy one.

Paolo was an angry man, and he let his anger drive him to hurt his family. He treated Rita very badly and did not stay true to her as a husband. Rita prayed for the patience to endure these trials. Eventually, her virtues of kindness and compassion started to soften her husband's hard heart. Rita was particularly saddened by a violent feud between her husband's family and their rivals, the Chiqui family. The Mancini and the Chiqui families were constantly fighting back and forth. Finally, at her request, Paolo renounced the feud (which was called "The Vendetta") and sought peace.

His enemies, however, were not ready to forgive. Paolo was betrayed and killed by a member of the Chiqui family. At his funeral, Rita forgave the murderers and begged for peace. But Paolo's brother Bernardo wanted revenge. Bernardo began trying to convince Rita's sons, Giovanni Antonio and Paolo Maria, to seek bloody vengeance for their father's death.

Rita could not bear the thought of her sons becoming men of violence, as their father had once been. She prayed that the young men would not join in "The Vendetta." When they died of illness a year later, her grief was tempered by the consolation that God had preserved her sons from committing the sin of murder.

Having lost both her husband and her sons, Rita returned to her dream of joining a convent. But the sisters were worried about her joining them due to her connection to the violent feud. The decision was that she

could join the convent only if she could reconcile her husband's family and their bitter rivals. Rita prayed and asked for the intercession of three patron saints: Saint John the Baptist, Saint Augustine, and Saint Nicholas of Tolentino. The saints must have helped her, as Rita convinced the rival families, even her brother-in-law Bernardo, to put aside their hatred. Then she finally joined the Augustinian sisters of the convent of Saint Mary Magdalene.

Rita lived a life of prayer and penance in the convent. When she was sixty years old, she received a strange gift: a small wound appeared on her forehead and would not heal. It was as if a thorn from Jesus' crown of thorns had marked her. This wound was on Rita's forehead for the rest of her life and remained visible after she died. It might have been a sign of how Rita kept Jesus' Passion always at the forefront of her mind.

When Rita was near the end of her life and confined to bed, she received another gift. She asked a visiting cousin to bring her a rose from the garden of her old home. Even though it was a cold January and no roses would be in bloom, the cousin checked—and found a single rose, miraculously alive! She brought it back to Rita. The holy woman accepted the rose, as she had accepted the thorn mark, with love.

Two hundred years later, long after Rita's death, bees appeared at the convent of Saint Mary Magdalene. This swarm of bees built a hive in the walls of the building. They are said to live there still, hibernating for most of the year but emerging during Holy Week and disappearing back into the wall on Saint Rita's feast day, May 22. These bees are colored like normal bees, but they have no stingers. The sisters love the bees because they serve as a reminder of the sweetness and peace that Saint Rita embodied in the midst of the buzzing clamor of the noisy world.

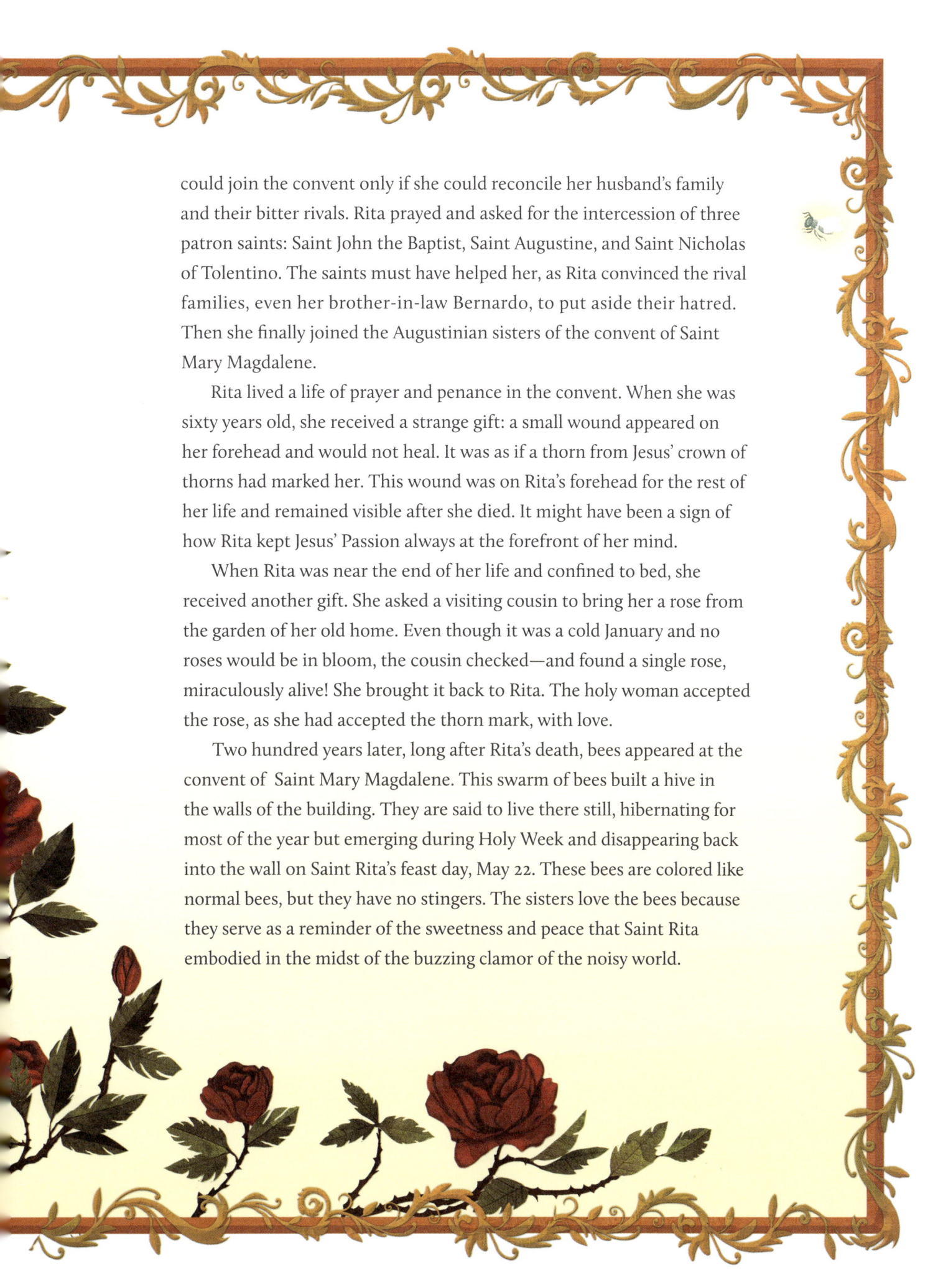

The Hyena and Saint Macarius

The sun beat down on the Egyptian desert. A single hyena made her way across the burning sands to a cave. She pawed at the stony cave mouth, as if knocking on a door. When she received no reply, she cautiously slunk inside.

The cave had been made into a monk's simple dwelling-place, with a bare wooden cot and a few books and icons. In the middle of the space, an old, thin monk knelt. He was so deep in prayer that he did not notice his unusual visitor. The hyena came closer to the man and began to lick his feet.

The monk turned to the creature and blinked in confusion. Why had this hyena come to interrupt his prayers? The hyena redoubled her efforts to communicate. She tugged gently at the monk's tunic with her teeth. Now he could see the animal was clearly in distress. He arose from his knees and followed her.

Monk and beast walked through the desert. The hyena led the man to another cave and disappeared inside. She emerged back into the sunlight carrying a hyena cub in her mouth, and she set it down in front of the monk. She returned to the cave twice, bringing out two more cubs. The monk could tell from their milky eyes that all three cubs were blind.

Finally, he understood what the mother hyena wanted from him. One by one, he lifted up each hyena pup and prayed over it. For each cub, he moistened his finger with spit and traced the sign of the cross over its eyes. When he had completed his prayers, the hyena cubs began blinking and looking around in delighted surprise. Their blindness had been cured! The mother hyena laughed in gratitude.

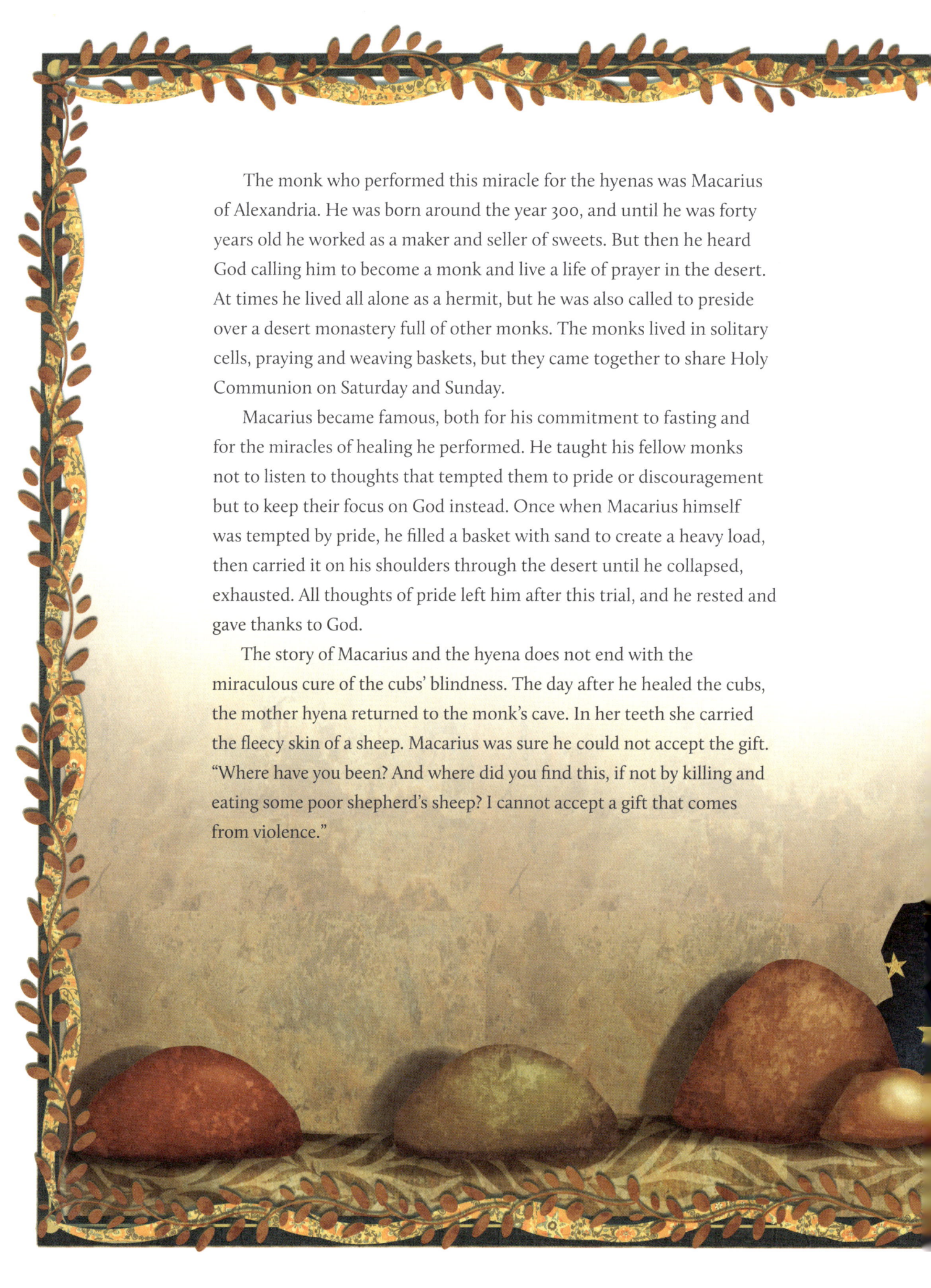

The monk who performed this miracle for the hyenas was Macarius of Alexandria. He was born around the year 300, and until he was forty years old he worked as a maker and seller of sweets. But then he heard God calling him to become a monk and live a life of prayer in the desert. At times he lived all alone as a hermit, but he was also called to preside over a desert monastery full of other monks. The monks lived in solitary cells, praying and weaving baskets, but they came together to share Holy Communion on Saturday and Sunday.

Macarius became famous, both for his commitment to fasting and for the miracles of healing he performed. He taught his fellow monks not to listen to thoughts that tempted them to pride or discouragement but to keep their focus on God instead. Once when Macarius himself was tempted by pride, he filled a basket with sand to create a heavy load, then carried it on his shoulders through the desert until he collapsed, exhausted. All thoughts of pride left him after this trial, and he rested and gave thanks to God.

The story of Macarius and the hyena does not end with the miraculous cure of the cubs' blindness. The day after he healed the cubs, the mother hyena returned to the monk's cave. In her teeth she carried the fleecy skin of a sheep. Macarius was sure he could not accept the gift. "Where have you been? And where did you find this, if not by killing and eating some poor shepherd's sheep? I cannot accept a gift that comes from violence."

The hyena bowed her head low and whined, as if imploring Macarius to accept what she had brought. The monk said, in a softer voice, "I see you have brought me what you could out of gratitude. I will relent and take it, on one condition: promise me you will not vex the poor by eating their sheep. If you are hungry, come hither to me for bread." The hyena nodded her head up and down eagerly, and Macarius was satisfied.

From then on, the hyena would come to Macarius' cave when she could not find food, and the monk would share his bread with her. And the old monk slept on the sheepskin, the gift of a grateful mother hyena, for the rest of his days.

The Ravens and Saint Meinrad

A pair of black-feathered baby birds cawed plaintively from a nest in the deep, dark woods. For reasons they did not understand, their mother had not returned to feed them in a long time, and their tiny stomachs were aching with hunger. But in the depths of the forest, no one was likely to hear the orphaned birds except a predator who might gobble them up, like a great brown bear. Still, calling for help was all the little birds could do, and so they cawed with all their might.

And it was not a bear that heard their cries. Instead, a man in a black robe approached their nest, leaning on a traveling staff. He listened to the distressed cries of the young ravens. Then, he looked down at what he held in his hand: his prized possession, a statue of the Virgin Mary. The Virgin held her young son, Jesus, and perched on the Child Jesus' hand was a tiny, carved bird. The man smiled with understanding. He tucked the statue into his belt and used both hands to tenderly scoop up the ravens' nest.

The ravens' new friend was Meinrad. He had been born to a noble family in the late 700s in what is now Germany. He was educated at an island abbey in the middle of Lake Constance. Preferring the simple life of the abbey to the life of a noble, he entered the Benedictine order as a monk. Eventually, he was also ordained a priest.

Above all, Meinrad valued solitary time in prayer. He got permission from his monastic superiors to withdraw to a hermitage where he could focus entirely on God. He set out from the island abbey in a flat-bottomed boat and sailed for a mountain on the far side of the lake, a mountain covered in deep, dark woods. He took with him only a few necessities and his most cherished possession, a statue of the Virgin Mary that he had received as a gift from his friend Abbess Hildegard of Zurich.

Meinrad was just beginning his life as a hermit when he discovered and adopted the two ravens. He fed them by hand until they learned to fly and find food for themselves. To the forlorn birds, he must have seemed like a savior sent by God. And perhaps God also put the ravens in his life so that this solitary priest would not be so very alone on earth, despite his seclusion. They had another role to play as well, at the end of Meinrad's life: bringing a pair of wicked men to justice.

Meinrad wished for solitude, but he also offered hospitality to travelers who passed by his hermitage. Soon he gained a reputation for holiness, and more and more pilgrims came specifically to visit him, bringing gifts and requesting prayers. Meinrad agreed to pray but turned down the gifts. After seven years he decided to find greater seclusion deeper in the woods and further from pilgrims. He brought with him the carved Mary and the two birds, now grown.

Deep in the forest, with mighty pine trees on all sides, Meinrad found a bubbling spring. He settled there and built for himself a log hut and little chapel. He set up his statue and a simple crucifix, and the ravens would often perch on either side of the cross.

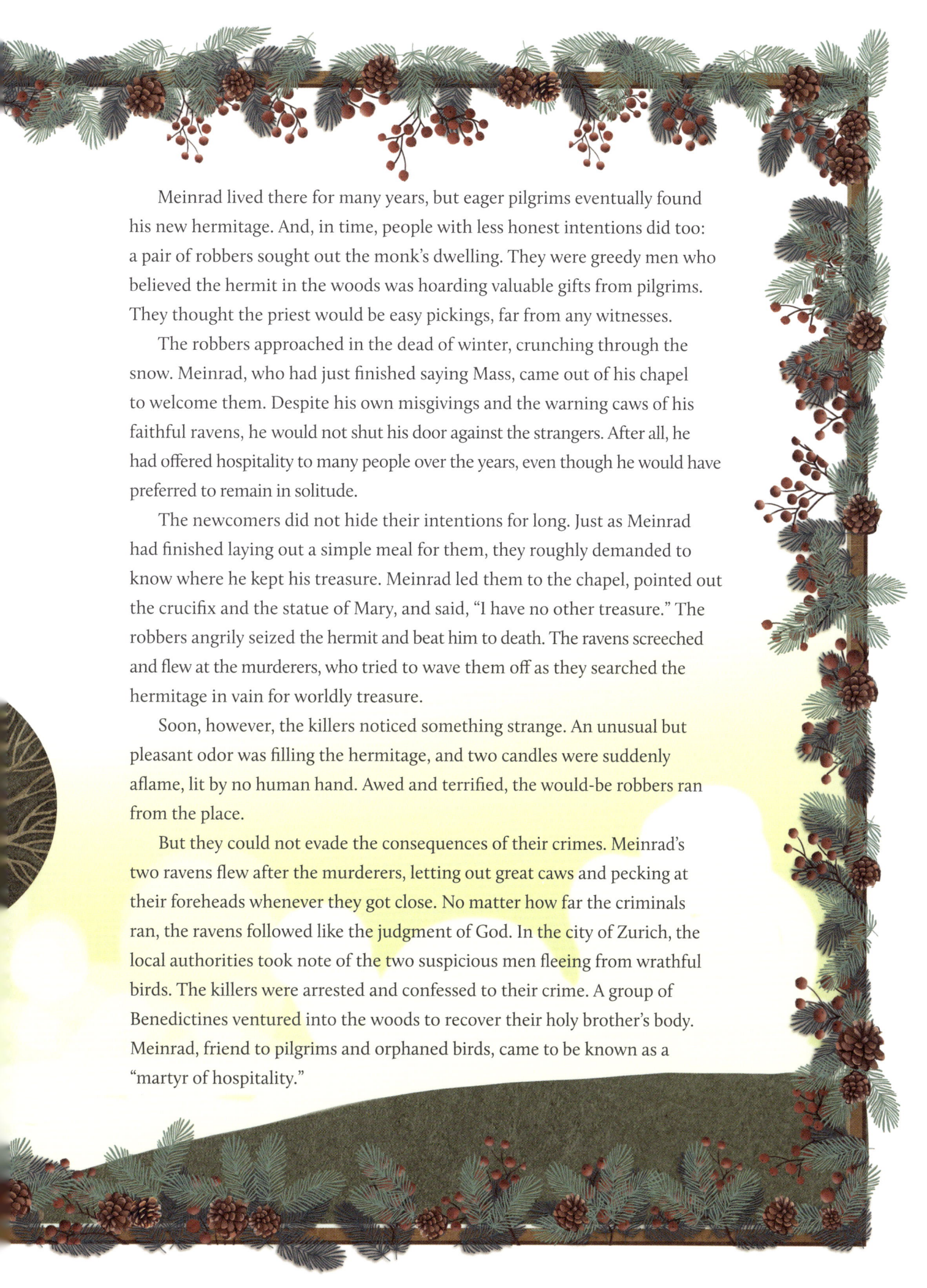

Meinrad lived there for many years, but eager pilgrims eventually found his new hermitage. And, in time, people with less honest intentions did too: a pair of robbers sought out the monk's dwelling. They were greedy men who believed the hermit in the woods was hoarding valuable gifts from pilgrims. They thought the priest would be easy pickings, far from any witnesses.

The robbers approached in the dead of winter, crunching through the snow. Meinrad, who had just finished saying Mass, came out of his chapel to welcome them. Despite his own misgivings and the warning caws of his faithful ravens, he would not shut his door against the strangers. After all, he had offered hospitality to many people over the years, even though he would have preferred to remain in solitude.

The newcomers did not hide their intentions for long. Just as Meinrad had finished laying out a simple meal for them, they roughly demanded to know where he kept his treasure. Meinrad led them to the chapel, pointed out the crucifix and the statue of Mary, and said, "I have no other treasure." The robbers angrily seized the hermit and beat him to death. The ravens screeched and flew at the murderers, who tried to wave them off as they searched the hermitage in vain for worldly treasure.

Soon, however, the killers noticed something strange. An unusual but pleasant odor was filling the hermitage, and two candles were suddenly aflame, lit by no human hand. Awed and terrified, the would-be robbers ran from the place.

But they could not evade the consequences of their crimes. Meinrad's two ravens flew after the murderers, letting out great caws and pecking at their foreheads whenever they got close. No matter how far the criminals ran, the ravens followed like the judgment of God. In the city of Zurich, the local authorities took note of the two suspicious men fleeing from wrathful birds. The killers were arrested and confessed to their crime. A group of Benedictines ventured into the woods to recover their holy brother's body. Meinrad, friend to pilgrims and orphaned birds, came to be known as a "martyr of hospitality."

The Lion and Saint Mary of Egypt

The desert stretched on for miles, as far as the eye could see. A lion walked through the desert, moving slowly but surely toward the only other creatures in sight. An old priest was weeping over a lifeless woman, her body lying on the sand with her hands folded peacefully. She was wrapped in a tattered cloak, her skin was tan and wrinkled, and her hair was bleached by the desert sun. The priest brought his tear-stained face down to reverently kiss the dead woman's feet. He was so full of grief that he did not notice the lion nearby.

For a little while, the lion listened to the priest weeping. Then the priest got to his feet and began to chant—he was reciting Psalms and prayers for the woman, conducting a solitary funeral. But when the time came to bury the body, the priest hesitated. It was as if he was wondering if he was worthy to lay her body to rest.

Only then did the priest look down to see a message traced into the sand near the woman's head. "Father Zosima, bury on this spot the body of humble Mary. Return to dust that which is dust and pray to the Lord for me." As the lion watched, the priest set to work. But soon he stopped again, trying to catch his breath. He did not have the strength to dig the grave. He tried using a scrap of wood as a shovel, but the ground was dry and hard, and he could barely make a dent in it. Searching for something else with which to dig, he turned and finally saw the lion.

Father Zosima froze in fear, face to face with the great, maned lion. How had he found himself alone in the desert with a dead woman and a wild beast? It was all because of the extraordinary story of Mary of Egypt.

Mary of Egypt's own life was just as surprising and mysterious as the lion who arrived at her desert funeral. Father Zosima had heard her story two years before, when he first met the woman while he wandered in the desert as a Lenten penance. She knew his name before he told it, and once when she prayed he saw her rise up from the ground and hover in the air. Thinking he had found a saint, he begged to know the story of her life.

Mary's story was one of dramatic conversion. She was born in Egypt in the mid-300s. At the age of twelve, she ran away from home. She came to the city of Alexandria and lived a life of sin, addicted to pleasure-seeking and careless of her soul. She mocked and despised those who lived holy lives. She even went on a pilgrimage to Jerusalem in order to tempt other pilgrims to vice. But something happened in Jerusalem that changed everything.

Mary tried to enter a church where pilgrims were venerating a relic of the Holy Cross, but an invisible force stopped her from entering. The rest of the crowd streamed in, leaving Mary standing by the door in confusion. Again she tried, and again, and again . . . but each time the same unseen power blocked her way. She retreated to a corner, pondering this mystery, and realized that it was her sinful life that stopped her from entering the church. She began to weep from guilt, until she looked up and saw an icon of the Virgin Mary, Mother of Jesus Christ.

"O Lady, Mother of God," she cried. "I know I am unworthy. But I have heard that your Son came to call sinners to repentance. Help me, for I have no other help. Let the church entrance be opened for me so I can look on the

Holy Cross, where your Son shed his blood for sinners—for me, unworthy as I am. I promise as soon as I see it, I will turn from my sins, renounce the world and its temptations, and go wherever you will lead me."

Mary's prayer was answered. She found she could now enter the church and look upon the Cross. And she was as good as her promise, following the lead of the Virgin Mary. On her way out of the church she looked at the same icon and heard a voice saying, "If you cross the Jordan, you will find glorious rest." She set out for the Jordan River, stopping at a monastery to confess her sins and receive absolution before setting out into the desert to live a life of prayer and penance.

After many years of prayerful solitude, she met Father Zosima on his Lenten journey and asked him to come back the next year on Holy Thursday to bring her Holy Communion. When he found her, she was on the opposite side of the river, but she calmly walked across the Jordan to receive the Eucharist. It was when he returned the year after that he found her body—and the lion.

As Father Zosima watched, the lion lowered its head to the saint's feet and began to lick them. The old priest crossed himself and prayed. The big lion seemed to be honoring the saint just as Father Zosima himself had done when he wept over her feet. Could her holiness have tamed the wildness of this beast? Gathering his courage, Father Zosima addressed the lion: "This great saint ordered that her body was to be buried. But I am old, and not strong enough to dig the grave. Can you carry out the work with your great claws? Then we can commit to the earth the mortal remains of the saint."

The lion nodded its mighty head and began to dig a grave with its massive paws, easily scooping away the dirt that the priest had struggled to move. Priest and lion together buried the saint, the priest offering prayers, the lion moving the desert earth. When the task was done, Father Zosima set out to tell his monastery about the saint's death, and the lion set off into the desert, as gentle as a lamb.

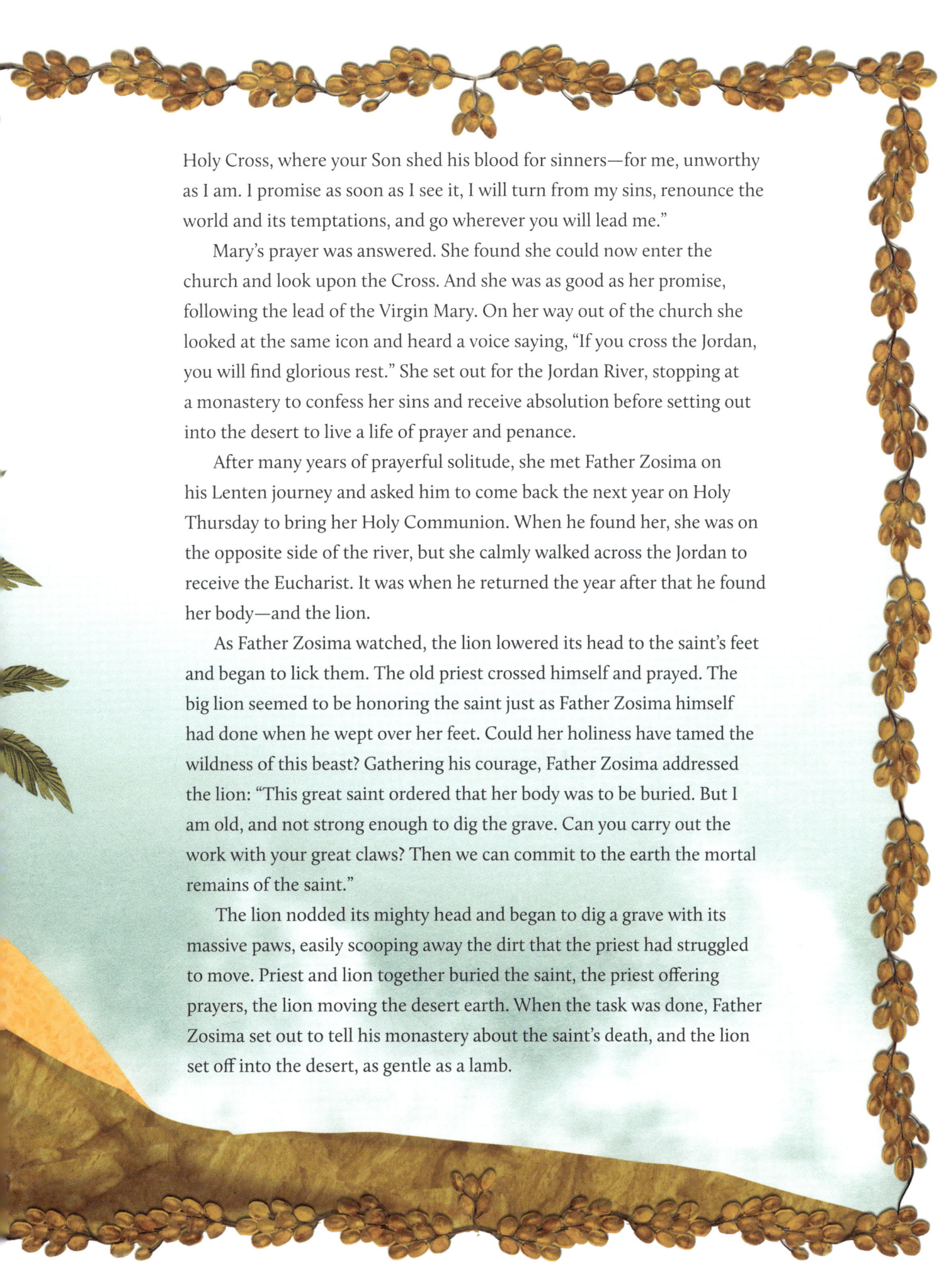

The Whale and Saint Brendan

The waters of the North Atlantic were choppy and rough. A boat was sailing those waters, crewed by men in brown robes—seventeen monks on a voyage of faith. "Look! Up ahead, there's an island," called out one monk. And indeed, a rugged promontory rose out of the sea before them. Though there was no easy place to dock the ship, the monks dropped anchor and swam through shallow water to the island, grateful for a respite from sailing, especially as darkness was falling.

One monk, their leader, stayed aboard the boat, deep in prayer all night long. The other men explored the island. It seemed uninhabited, even by plant life. They slept curled up on the ground, and when dawn came they celebrated Mass—Easter Sunday Mass, in fact. For reasons they would learn later, their abbot and captain remained in the boat, saying his own Mass.

The men gathered driftwood and brought out some salted meat and fish from their supplies. Soon they had a fire burning and a cookpot boiling. And then something strange happened. The island beneath their feet began to move like a wave. Suddenly it did not feel like solid rock at all! They rushed to rejoin their leader where he waited for them on the boat. He calmly helped the panicking monks aboard, and they all watched in astonishment as the island swam away. They could see their little fire getting smaller and smaller as the island carried it off, until it was just a pinprick of light.

The abbot, Brendan, addressed his crew of monks. "Brothers, you are wondering what has happened to this island." The monks mumbled fearfully, and Brendan said, "Fear not! God has revealed to me the mystery so I would be ready to get you aboard. This was no island, but a sea creature, the largest one in the ocean. It is so long that, try as it might, it cannot bring its head and tail together. Its name is Jasconius."

Believe it or not, this was not the wildest adventure Brendan would have. Brendan had been born in Munster, a province in the southwest of Ireland. He lived a long life from the late 400s to the late 500s. He was one of a group of missionaries called the Apostles of Ireland, who continued Saint Patrick's work of spreading the faith through the whole country. Brendan founded several monasteries and, in the process, voyaged to places nearby Ireland like the Aran Islands, the country of Wales, and Brittany on the northern coast of France. But his greatest voyage came when he was an old man.

The story goes that a priest named Barinthus told Brendan of a wondrous island he had visited: "The Promised Land of the Saints," something like a small reflection of heaven on earth. Brendan, then over eighty-six years old, fasted and prayed for forty days, asking God whether he should seek out this place. Sensing God's approval, Brendan and a crew of his monks built a traditional Irish boat out of woven branches and oxhide. They set sail for the Promised Land.

Legend has it that Brendan's voyage brought many marvelous sights: massive sheep, larger than oxen; sea serpents breathing fire; an island full of snow-white birds who sang Psalms with human voices. The monks were at sea for seven years.

Were they lost all that time? No, Brendan was just following God's directions. The voyage was something of a seafaring pilgrimage, one that required the monks to observe the yearly cycle of holy days. Every year they would return to spend Holy Saturday night and Easter Sunday morning on the back of their new friend, the great whale named Jasconius. As if to remind them of their first visit, the second time they landed on Jasconius they found the cookpot they had left before. Now that they knew the true nature of the island, they were careful not to alarm the whale that way again!

In the seventh year of their voyage, they returned once more to Jasconius for Easter. This time things were different. When they finished Easter Sunday Mass, the whole island began to move beneath them. The monks cried out to God in alarm, but Brendan reassured them: "Fear not. No evil shall befall us. Here we have only a helper on our journey."

Brendan was right. Jasconius the whale bore the monks safely to another island, where they found a guide who could bring them to the Promised Land of the Saints. Their voyage brought them to that beautiful island they had sought so faithfully. After some time exploring its marvels, they sailed home to their monastery, bringing stories of all the wonders God had shown them—including the great whale Jasconius.

The Pets of Blessed Carlo Acutis

Assorted barks and mews echoed through the elegant Italian home. A boy in his early teens chased his dogs and cats around, video camera in hand. The pets loved playing with the energetic boy, the only child of his family. The boy loved the animals right back. He also liked to amuse his friends with videos of his dogs and cats, using his computer to dub silly voice-overs on the pet footage.

Does this sound like the story of a saint to you? You might be surprised to meet these pets and their young playmate, after hearing stories of saints from the more distant past who interacted with animals you have only seen in zoos: lions and tigers, hyenas and wolves.

But these Italian house pets were friends with a saint as well. The pets were four dogs named Briciola, Stellina, Chiara, and Poldo, and two cats named Bambi and Cleopatra. (The house was also home to a number of goldfish over the years.) And their friend was Carlo Acutis: an ordinary boy, but also a friend of Jesus who now intercedes for us with his prayers.

Carlo was born in 1991. His wealthy parents moved from London, England, to Milan, Italy, shortly after he was born. As Carlo grew up, he developed into a friendly and kind young man with many varied interests, from soccer to Spider-Man to computer programming—and, of course, his beloved pets. He was also, to his parents' surprise, devoted to Jesus Christ.

Carlo had been baptized as a baby, but his parents were not very religious and did not take him to church. When he started to have questions about God and the faith, it was his Polish Catholic babysitter who answered them. She helped nurture Carlo's interest in God, and soon he convinced his parents to bring him to church regularly. First his mother, then his father, became practicing Catholics, pulled along by young Carlo's love for the Church.

Carlo was especially devoted to Jesus in the Holy Eucharist. He asked for and was given permission to receive First Holy Communion at age seven, earlier than was customary in Milan, and he began receiving the Eucharist regularly. As he grew older, he was inspired to use his talent with computers to spread devotion to the Holy Eucharist. Carlo was sad that so few people attended Mass or Adoration. He wanted more people to understand how Jesus is present in the Sacrament, so he created a website to document every time a Eucharistic miracle occurred—every time Jesus' Body and Blood became miraculously visible in the Sacrament.

Carlo led a busy life! He did all the things you would expect for a boy his age—hanging out and making jokes with friends, teaching himself skills like computer coding, playing with his cats and dogs. But he did a few things that went beyond that: he defended classmates who were picked on because of their disabilities, and he offered kindness to kids going through difficulties in their family life. He did volunteer work to help the poor and hungry, and he saved up his allowance to buy a sleeping bag for a homeless man he knew. And he centered his life on Jesus, going to Mass and Adoration each day and asking his parents to bring him on pilgrimages to places where there had been Eucharistic miracles or where Mary had appeared to people.

When Carlo was fifteen, he suddenly became seriously ill with blood cancer. In the hospital, Carlo offered up his suffering for the pope and the

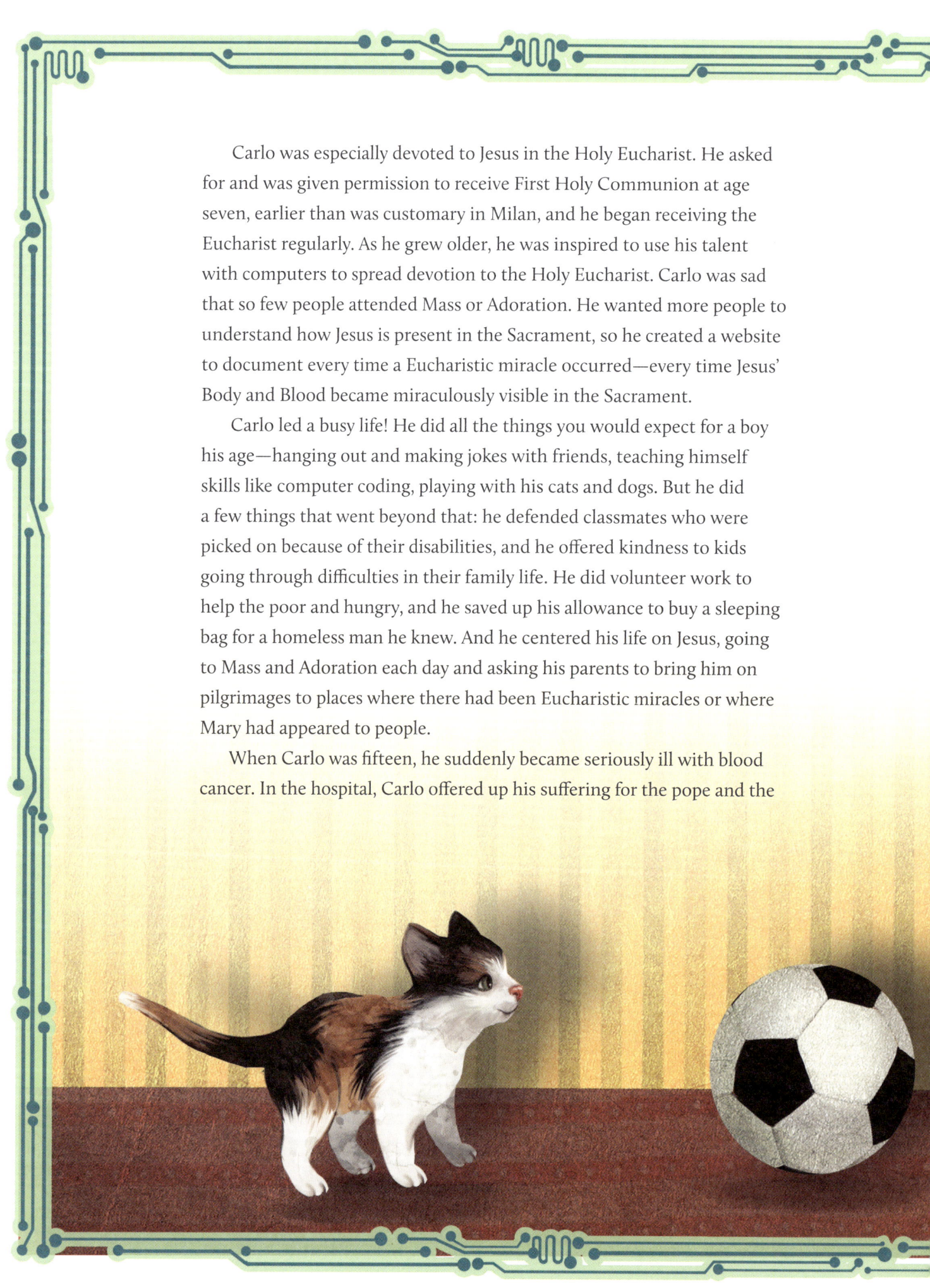

Church. He comforted his mother by telling her, "I can die happy because I haven't wasted even a minute on things that aren't pleasing to God."

After his death, people quickly began asking the Church to look into whether this ordinary young man with an extraordinary love for God was a saint. His story shows us that holiness is possible—for each of us, right now!

On his website about Eucharistic miracles, Carlo offered rules for how to become holy. His number one rule was this: "You must want it with all your heart." And he lived this rule out. Yes, he loved video games and soccer, cats and dogs, and you can love those things, too. But God was Carlo's first and foremost love. He understood how to give thanks to God by cherishing the good things God made, like his animal friends. By giving God his heart, he learned the best way to love the wonderful world God made.

Sources

"The Wolf and Saint Francis of Assisi" inspired by *The Little Flowers of Saint Francis of Assisi*, trans. Abby Langdon Alger (Boston: Little, Brown, & Co., 1887), 93–99.

"The Whale and Saint Brendan" inspired by *Brendaniana: St. Brendan the Voyager in Story and Legend*, written by Denis O'Donoghue, 2nd ed. (Dublin: Browne & Nolan, 1895), 111–178.

Acknowledgements

Special thanks to Meg Hunter-Kilmer for sharing her knowledge and love for the saints and to Fr. Philip Yang and his mother Helen Yang for translating Korean sources of the story of Blessed James Heo In-baek.